NO LONGER PROPERTY OF
ANYTHINK LIBRARIES/
RANGEVIEW LIBRARY DISTRICT

D1505915

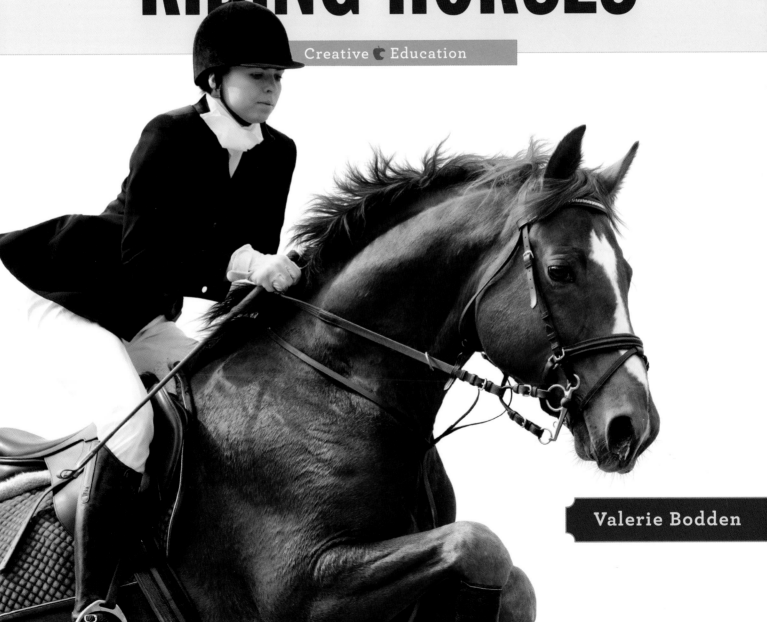

HORSING AROUND

# RIDING HORSES

Creative Education

Valerie Bodden

*Published by* Creative Education
P.O. Box 227, Mankato, Minnesota 56002
Creative Education is an imprint of
The Creative Company
www.thecreativecompany.us

*Design and production by* Chelsey Luther
*Art direction by* Christine Vanderbeek
*Printed in* the United States of America

*Photographs by* Dreamstime (Kseniya Abramova,
Convisum, Justek16, Sawitri Khromkrathok, Richard
Lammerts), Shutterstock (Cattallina, holbox, Charles
Knowles, Abramova Kseniya, Jim Noetzel, pirita, Kiselev
Andrew Valerevich, Ventura), SuperStock (age fotostock,
Cultura Limited, Exactostock)

Copyright © 2014 Creative Education
*International copyright reserved in all countries.*
*No part of this book may be reproduced in any form*
*without written permission from the publisher.*

Library of Congress Cataloging-in-Publication Data
Bodden, Valerie.
Riding horses / Valerie Bodden
p. cm. — (Horsing around)
*Summary:* A narrative guide to riding horses, from where
to ride the animals, how to saddle them, how to mount
and give orders to them, and what to wear and expect as
you perform daily tasks.
Includes bibliographical references and index.
ISBN 978-1-60818-471-2
1. Horsemanship—Juvenile literature. 2. Horses—Juvenile
literature. I. Title.

SF309.2.B63 2013
636.1'3—dc23       2012049912


9 8 7 6 5 4 3

# TABLE OF CONTENTS

# RIDING OFF

You hold the **reins** in your hands. You feel the **stirrups** around your feet. You smile. There is nothing like riding a horse!

Riding a horse takes skill and patience.

# STARTING OUT

BEFORE you can ride a horse, you need to go up to it with **confidence**. Touch it lightly on the neck. You might even give your horse a treat!

Horses can tell when people are nervous or scared.

# WHERE TO GO

YOU can ride a horse in an indoor **arena**. Or you can ride it on trails outside. Some people ride in fields or along roads that are not too busy.

Some trails take riders past lakes and woods.

# SADDLED UP

TO get your horse ready to ride, you need to put a **saddle** on it. A **bridle** goes over the horse's head. It has a **bit** that goes into the horse's mouth. The bit is attached to the reins. The bit and reins help control the horse.

The headstall is the part of the bridle that fits over the ears.

# STEADY MOUNT

TO mount, or get on, your horse, you can use a stool. Or you can have someone help you up. Sit up straight in the saddle. Hold the reins in your hands.

Grab onto the side of the saddle when getting a boost up.

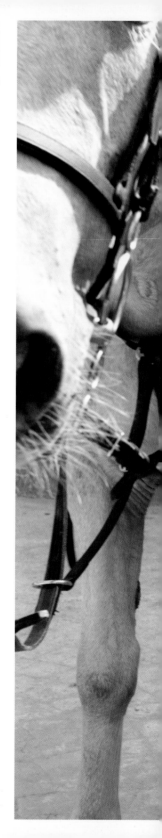

13

# GIVING ORDERS

WHEN you want your horse to walk, squeeze its sides with your legs. To make it stop, lean back a little bit in the saddle. Pull back gently on the reins. To turn right, hold the right rein out to the right side. Press the left rein into the horse's neck. Press your left leg into the horse's side.

How a rider sits on the saddle can tell the horse what to do.

# CHANGING SPEEDS

ONCE you have learned to ride your horse, you can go faster. You can learn to **trot** and **canter**. Then you can learn to **gallop**!

A horse can run as fast as 25 to 30 miles (40–48 km) per hour.

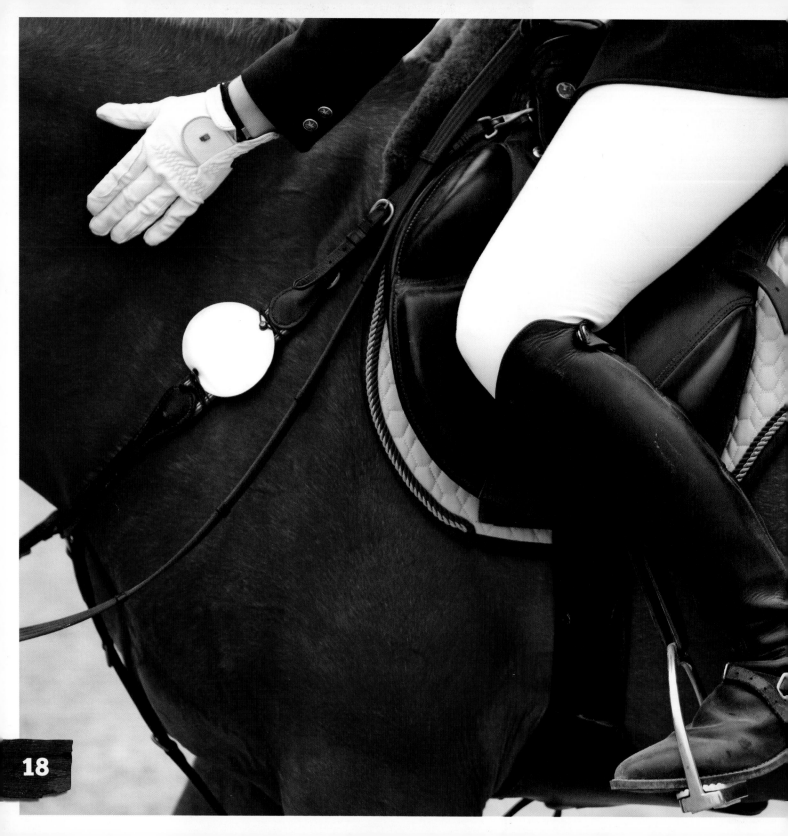

# WHAT TO WEAR

You need to wear a helmet when you are training your horse. Boots keep your feet from getting stepped on. Gloves keep your hands from getting rope burn.

Metal parts called spurs stick out from riding boots.

# THE END OF THE DAY

WHEN you are done riding, **groom** your horse. Clean your **tack** with a sponge and saddle soap. Then think about the next time you can ride. The more you ride your horse, the happier it will be!

Many different brushes are used in grooming a horse.

# HORSE DICTIONARY

**arena**: a large building with lots of space for riding horses

**bit**: part of a bridle that is usually made out of metal and fits into a horse's mouth

**bridle**: straps that go over a horse's head and hold a bit and reins

**canter**: a way of moving in which a horse keeps the legs on one side of its body in front of the legs on the other side

**confidence**: feeling brave and sure, not scared

**gallop**: a way of moving in which a horse runs by moving each foot separately

**groom**: to clean an animal's fur or coat

**reins**: straps that run from the bit to the rider's hands so that the rider can use them to control the horse

**saddle**: a seat that is strapped onto a horse's back

**stirrups**: metal rings that hang down from a saddle and are used to hold the rider's feet

**tack**: the equipment, such as saddles, bridles, and reins, used when riding a horse

**trot**: a way of moving in which a horse moves the front foot on one side of its body at the same time as the back foot on the other side

# READ MORE

De la Bédoyère, Camilla. *Horses and Ponies*. Irvine, Calif.: QEB, 2010.

Pipe, Jim. *Horses*. North Mankato, Minn.: Stargazer Books, 2007.

Ransford, Sandy. *Learn to Ride*. Irvine, Calif.: QEB Publishing, 2011.

# WEBSITES

**Enchanted Learning: Horse Printout**
*http://www.enchantedlearning.com/subjects/mammals/horse/Horsecoloring.shtml*
Learn more about the parts of a horse, and print a picture of a horse to color.

**Horses 4 Gaits**
*http://www.youtube.com/watch?v=ifKU_kVQhd4*
Watch a horse walk, trot, canter, and gallop.

*Every effort has been made to ensure that these sites are suitable for children, that they have educational value, and that they contain no inappropriate material. However, because of the nature of the Internet, it is impossible to guarantee that these sites will remain active indefinitely or that their contents will not be altered.*